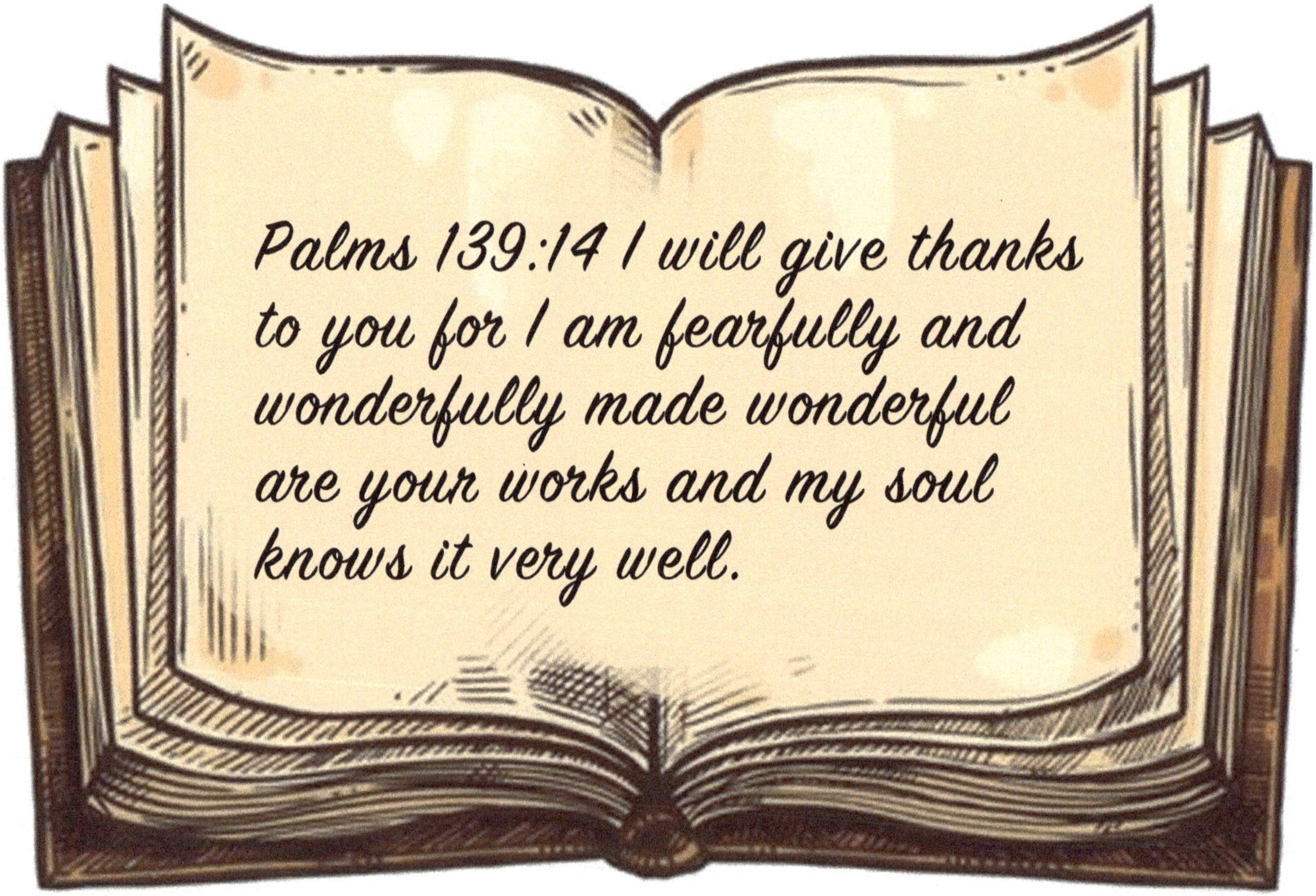
Palms 139:14 I will give thanks
to you for I am fearfully and
wonderfully made wonderful
are your works and my soul
knows it very well.

In Loving Memory of

Spc. Abigail Rose Jenks

November 18, 2000 - April 19, 2021

"Every day may not be a good day;
but there is something good in every day." - Abby

As long as there is someone in the sky to protect me, there is no one on earth who can break me!

-Abby

Have you ever seen a parrot

who's best friend was a ferret?

The parrot loved to fly so high almost touching the sky.

The ferret said: "I wish I could fly that high and touch the sky."

The parrot said: "You can't fly, you're not that kind of guy."

"You need to scamper around
and stay down on the ground."

The ferret said:
"Will you teach me to fly
so I can go high?"

The parrot said: "Put on this cape and we will escape!"

So he put on the cape
and the parrot grabbed
hold hang on tight:
"This is your first flight."

The parrot and ferret took flight
and soared all through the night.

When they landed on the ground
the ferret scampered all around.

The ferret said:
"It was nice to fly so high,
but you were right,
I'm really not that kind of guy!"

The parrot said:
"See? Everyday is a good day
as long as we can play!"

Have you ever seen
a parrot and a ferret flying high
up in the beautiful night sky?

John 3:16 for God so loved the
world that he gave his only son
that who ever believes in him will
not perish but go to live in heaven
with him forever.

For Jenny, Emily and Esther;

Jack and Bump;

and binmen around the world.

It's early in the morning when you hardly hear a sound,
except for binman Benny as he whistles on his round.

He rides his truck from house to house and empties every bin
and all the time he does it, he wears a massive grin.

Can it be because he loves a morning in the sun?
Or a joke his friend has told that's causing all the fun?

It's because he's found a toaster that someone threw away,
which he needs to finish building something at his home today.

A DRAGON!

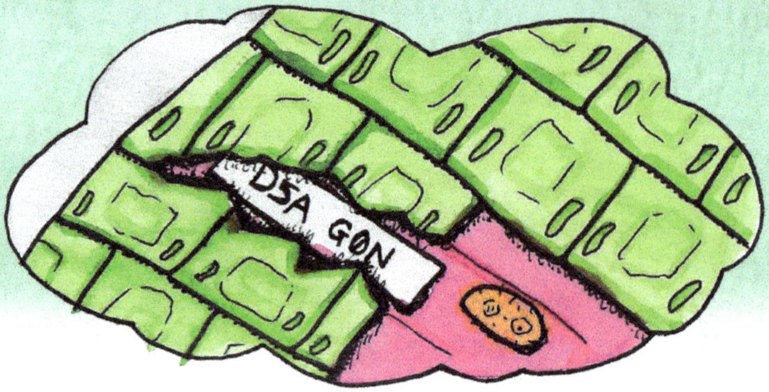

Its head is a shopping trolley, its body is a car,

its tail is made of cables and its legs are iron bars.

The dragon's scales are bin lids, its claws are made of wire,

and Benny needs a toaster to make it breathe out fire.

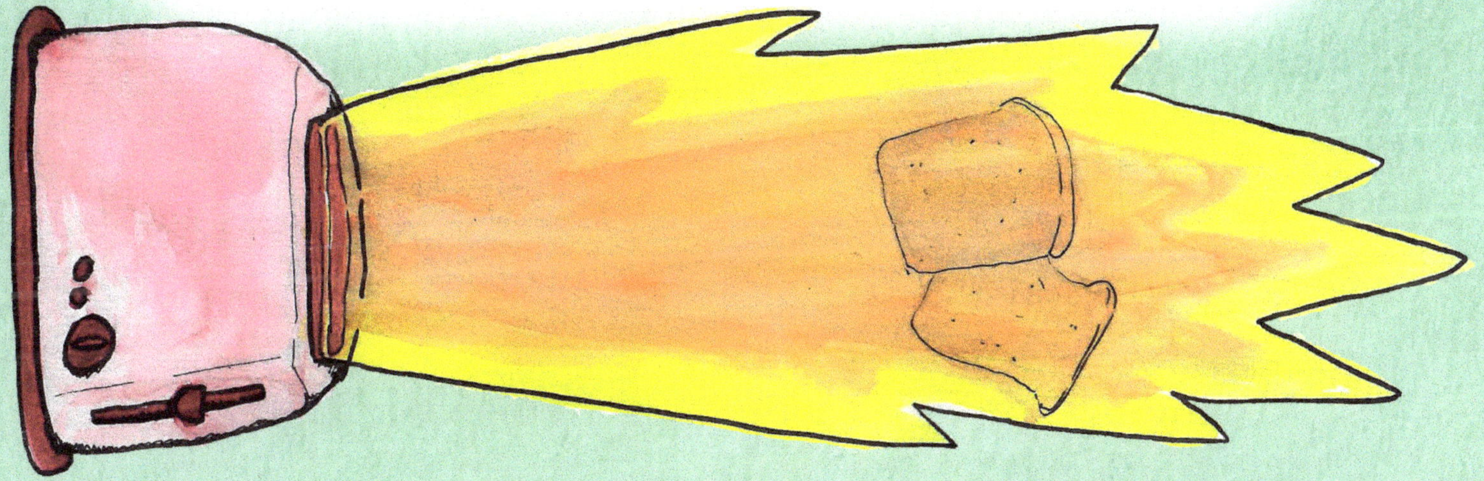

Its big black wings of bin bags lift it to the sky
and dragon-builder Benny is flying very high.

But Benny lands his dragon so that he can read a text,
it's from his wife and daughter, who want to go up next.

CPSIA information can be obtained
at www.ICGtesting.com
Printed in the USA
BVHW020755240921
617399BV00029B/586

9 781527 296411